EARTH VS. MARS

T0062044

CHERRY LAKE PRESS

Published in the United States of America by Cherry Lake Publishing
Ann Arbor, Michigan
www.cherrylakepublishing.com

Reading Adviser: Beth Walker Gambro, MS, Ed., Reading Consultant, Yorkville, IL
Book Designer: Book Buddy Media
Photo Credits: Cover: ©NASA/nasa.gov; page 1: ©NASA/GSFC / nasa.gov; page 5: ©Terra >
MODIS / nasa.gov; page 7: ©NASA / nasa.gov; page 9: ©D1min / Shutterstock; page 10: ©Chip
Somodevilla / Staff / Getty Images; page 11: ©nasa.gov; page 13: ©NASA / Handout / Getty
Images; page 15: ©NASA/JPL-Caltech / nasa.gov; page 16: ©NASA/MSFC / nasa.gov; page 17:
©NASA/JPL / nasa.gov; page 19: ©NASA / nasa.gov; page 21: ©NASA/JPL-Caltech/MSSS /
nasa.gov; page 23: ©Nirian / Getty Images; page 25: ©nasa.gov; page 26: ©NASA/Langley /
nasa.gov; page 27: ©NASA/Langley / nasa.gov; page 29: © / nasa.gov; page 30: ©NASA
/ nasa.gov

Cherry Lake Press is an imprint of Cherry Lake Publishing Group.

Library of Congress Cataloging-in-Publication Data has been filed and is available
at catalog.loc.gov

Cherry Lake Publishing would like to acknowledge the work of the Partnership for
21st Century Learning, a Network of Battelle for Kids.
Please visit *http://www.battelleforkids.org/networks/p21* for more information.

Printed in the United States of America
Corporate Graphics

ABOUT THE AUTHOR

Mari Bolte is a children's book author and editor. Streaming sci-fi on TV is more her
speed but tracking our planet's progress across the sky is still exciting! She lives in
Minnesota with her husband, daughter, and a house full of (non-Martian) pets.

TABLE OF CONTENTS

Destination: Mars

Earth, sometimes called the Blue Planet, is more than 4.5 billion years old. The first modern humans date back to between 100,000 and 300,000 years ago. We have tried to understand both our own planet and others in our solar system for thousands of years. Over the last few centuries, our explorations have become more scientific. Around 60 years ago, we sent the first spacecraft beyond Earth's **orbit**. We have set our sights for the future on our next-door neighbor: Mars, the Red Planet.

Earth is the only known planet in our universe that supports life.

Like Earth, Mars is a terrestrial planet. This means it is rocky and has a solid **core**. It also has ice that could potentially be melted for water. And because it is close to the Sun, solar rays could be used as a source of power.

After Earth, Mars is the most-explored planet in the solar system. Nearly 50 spacecraft have been sent to study Mars since 1960. Around 40 percent of those actually reached the Red Planet. Every piece of information they sent back has given us hope that someday people will get there, too.

Game Day

Millions of people on Earth tune in to watch their favorite sports teams on television. Many others show up in person to see their team play in their home stadium. What if their home stadium was on Mars? Right now, stadiums across Earth are going green. Lincoln Financial Stadium, home of the Philadelphia Eagles, has more than 11,000 solar panels. For about a decade, it also used 14 wind turbines. Wind and solar are also possible power sources on Mars. Solar panels could collect electricity on clear days. Then wind turbines could do the same during dust storms, when solar collection is impossible.

The length of a day on Mars is very similar to a day on Earth. One day on Earth is 24 hours. One day on Mars is 24 hours, 39 minutes, and 35 seconds. This means both planets have a similar **rotation** as they circle the Sun. But Mars orbits the Sun more slowly, and it is about 49 million miles (79 million kilometers) farther away. One year here is 365 Earth days long. One year on Mars lasts 687 Earth days.

That's not the only difference between Earth and Mars. There is less gravity on the Red Planet. A 100-pound (45.4 kilograms) person on Earth would only weigh 38 pounds (17.2 kg) on Mars. What would you do with all that extra spring in your step?

You'd probably have to run straight to the coat store. The average temperature on Earth is around 57 degrees Fahrenheit (14 degrees Celsius). But on Mars, the average is –81°F (–63°C).

[21ST CENTURY SKILLS LIBRARY]

Cell phone towers, weather monitoring, digital television, emergency services, and online banking all rely on the 24 GPS satellites that orbit Earth.

Technological Advances

Space communication can benefit us, no matter what planet we are on. **Global Positioning System (GPS) navigation** was developed in the very earliest days of space exploration. Scientists noticed that Sputnik, a Russian **satellite** launched in 1957, gave off a radio signal. The signal got stronger the closer the satellite got to Earth, and weaker as it moved away. That led to the GPS technology we use today.

The same GPS that tells you how to get from your friend's house to the grocery store tells the International Space Station (ISS) which way it is facing and how fast it is going. It also helps scientists track spacecraft during rocket launches.

Traveling Through Space

The National Aeronautics and Space Administration (NASA) is building a spacecraft to send people farther into space. *Orion* will take astronauts farther than they have ever gone before, first to the Moon and then to Mars. Its test launch was made on December 5, 2014. It traveled 3,600 miles (5,794 km) above Earth. It took pictures from space.

Four hours after liftoff, *Orion* reentered Earth's atmosphere. It dropped into the ocean about 600 miles (966 km) off the coast of San Diego, California. It survived the 4,000°F (2,204°C) heat during reentry. It also withstood the high **radiation** astronauts would experience in deep space.

[21ST CENTURY SKILLS LIBRARY]

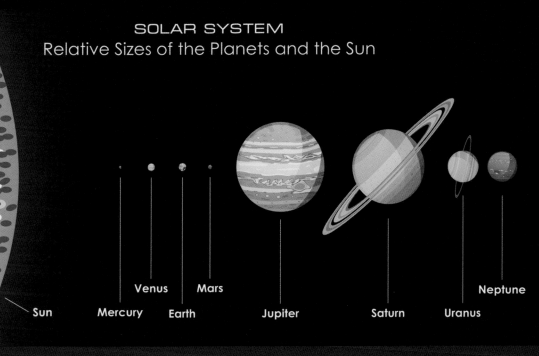

The spacecraft is scheduled to make its first **unmanned** test flight as part of the Artemis mission. The second stage, called Artemis 2, will take place with astronauts on board in 2023. Then Artemis 3 will take astronauts to the Moon in 2024.

Sending crews to **colonize** Mars is more than just spaceship development. The United States, Canada, Japan, and other countries are working to build their military presence in space. Much like each country having a naval force at sea, leaders around the world also want to be aware of issues and threats above the planet.

General John W. "Jay" Raymond previously served as the commander of the U.S. Space Command. Today he is the Chief of Space Operations for the U.S. Space Force.

Space Command is responsible for U.S. military operations in space. Space Command was created in 1985 but was shut down in 2002. It was reestablished in 2019. It protects America's interests in space, preventing conflicts, preparing for space combat, and providing power and defense to America and its allies. If requested, other branches of the military will offer assistance to Space Command.

[21ST CENTURY SKILLS LIBRARY]

Concordia Research Station is 372 miles (600 km) away from any other human life. This is around 120 miles (193 km) farther away than the ISS is from Earth.

Staying Warm

Understanding how the human body **adapts** to extreme cold is key to our future on Mars. For 2 decades, the European Space Agency (ESA) has sent a team to the Concordia Research Station in Antarctica. In winter, the team experiences Mars-like temperatures of up to –112°F (–80°C). Leaving and entering a habitat is time consuming. It also holds the risk of losing essential heat and introducing the risk of exposure to alien material. The ESA's Concordia project helps establish best practices for living in a new, unfamiliar, and frozen environment.

Jobs on Mars

Rovers have been examining rocks on Mars since Sojourner *landed in 1997. The types of rocks in a given place can tell scientists about the environmental conditions that the place has experienced. For example, some rocks are only formed in the presence of water. Although there is no known water on Mars now, finding those rocks shows us that there once was water there. Although rovers are equipped with the latest technology, there is no replacement for in-person fieldwork. Geologists could really dig in and uncover the secrets hidden under the surface of Mars.*

The U.S. Space Force is separate from Space Command. It is a newer branch of the military. It was formed in December 2019 and has its headquarters at the Pentagon in Washington, D.C. The Space Force operates and defends military satellites and ground stations used for communication and navigation, like GPS satellites. America has almost 1,900 satellites orbiting Earth. Space Force protects them.

The rover *Sojourner* could not rely on GPS communication on Mars. Instead, it used a technique called dead reckoning. It used what it knew about the direction and distance already traveled to calculate its current position.

It also monitors things that launch from Earth, including missiles. And it organizes, trains, and equips personnel to the U.S. Space Command. Like its sister organization, the U.S. Air Force, Space Force recruits young people to serve and go through basic training. Graduates wear special Space Force uniforms.

X Marks the Spot

NASA, Space Force, the ESA, and other agencies are working on getting humans safely into space. But what happens once astronauts have reached Mars? There will be some big adjustments between the Blue Planet and the Red Planet.

Earth is known as the Blue Planet because of its large amounts of water. Plants and animals on Earth need water. Humans need water. In fact, the human body is made up of around 60 percent water! But Mars is called the Red Planet. The planet's many rocks are full of iron. When iron **oxidizes**, it turns a rusty red color. Dust from rock **particles** enters the planet's atmosphere, turning the sky pink. That dusty surface

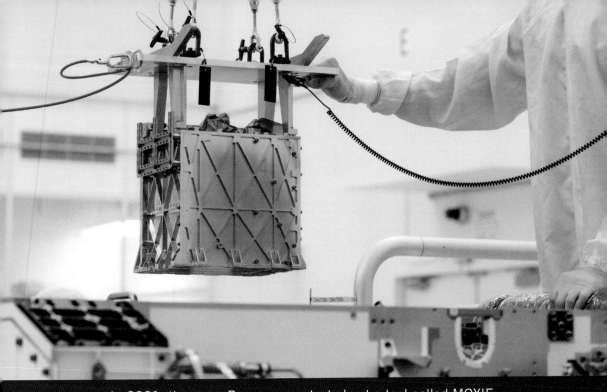

In 2021, the rover *Perseverance* tested out a tool called MOXIE. MOXIE is able to turn carbon dioxide molecules into oxygen.

has no known water sources. Finding a way to get or make water will be one of the first things colonists will need to do on Mars.

Another huge adjustment to life on Mars would be breathing. Earth's atmosphere is made of nitrogen, oxygen, argon, and trace amounts of other gases. The air on Earth has enough oxygen for us to breathe. Mars's atmosphere is mostly **carbon dioxide**, with a little water vapor mixed in. There are only trace amounts of oxygen on Mars.

The Environmental Control and Life Support System (ECLSS) provides clean air and water on the ISS. This model shows the shower, the waste management system, two water systems, and the oxygen generator.

The ISS has a water recycling program. It turns wastewater into drinkable water. It also recycles air to make oxygen. It makes between 5 and 20 pounds (2.3 and 9 kg) of oxygen a day, though. Just one human needs around 1.9 pounds (0.8 kg) of oxygen each day.

As a backup measure, shipments of oxygen are sent to the ISS from Earth. As an additional safety measure, there is an oxygen generator on board. But all of these methods rely on preexisting water, electricity, and extra deliveries. Being able to keep these supplies going on Mars will be essential to astronaut survival.

Neptune's winds travel more than 1,200 miles (2,000 km) per hour. Top wind speeds on Earth are only around 250 miles (400 km) per hour. This happened during a cyclone in 1996.

Neptune

Dark, cold, and windy, Neptune is the eighth planet in our solar system. At nearly 2.8 billion miles (4.6 billion km) away, it is also the farthest from the Sun. It cannot be seen through a telescope. And only one spacecraft, NASA's Voyager 2, has visited it up close. One day on Neptune takes about 16 Earth hours. A Neptunian year lasts about 165 Earth years. Fourteen moons and five rings circle the planet. Neptune is considered an ice giant because its mass is a hot, dense fluid of water, ammonia, and methane.

Exploring the Planet

Although we have not yet landed people on Mars, scientists have been exploring ways to prepare for that eventuality here on Earth. Finding ways to work, live, and move is nothing new. Designers have been making tiny houses, RVs, and trailers to **simulate** confined living spaces on the Moon and Mars for years. NASA's next generation of transportation is called the *Space Exploration Vehicle (SEV)*. Its design uses information gathered from the Apollo missions and the Mars rovers.

The *Space Exploration Vehicle* was tested at Arizona's Black Point Lava Flow in 2008.

The *SEV* is the size of a pickup truck—if that pickup had 12 wheels! Two astronauts can live aboard the *SEV* for up to 2 weeks. The pressurized cabin has space for beds and a bathroom. Moving at speeds of 6.2 miles (10 km) per hour, the astronauts can roll over rough or steep surfaces. Spacesuits are stored on the outside of the *SEV* and can be accessed through spaceports. Astronauts can be suited up for space walks in as little as 10 minutes.

Other Exploration

Around 3,500 years ago, ancient Polynesian people began sailing thousands of miles across the Pacific Ocean. Some studies hypothesize they sailed as far as North and South America. They brought livestock and plants along to help establish colonies. Their canoes were between 50 and 60 feet (15.2 and 18.3 meters) long and could carry 2 dozen people and their supplies. They were able to find their way by using the ocean waves, studying the flight patterns of birds, and locating stars in the sky.

A good spacesuit will keep astronauts safe from Mars's atmosphere. It will also protect their bodies from dangers. One such danger is space dust. On Earth, fine, soft dust in the air eventually ends up on the floor, where we vacuum or wipe it up. In space, static electricity causes dust to stick to things. And the dust on the Moon, and likely Mars, has sharp edges like glass that can hurt our bodies if we breathe it in.

Dust storms on Mars can cover the whole planet. The particles stick to everything, including solar panels. In 2018, a huge dust storm blocked the *Opportunity* rover's solar panels,

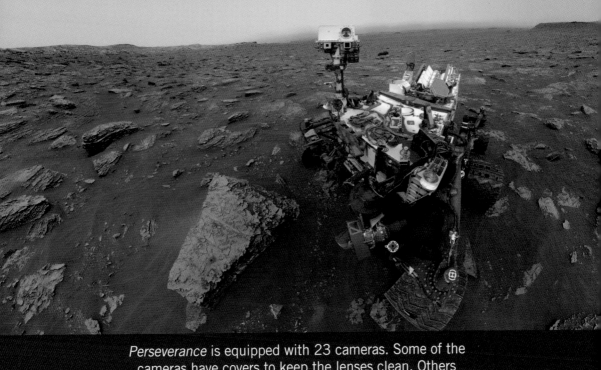

Perseverance is equipped with 23 cameras. Some of the cameras have covers to keep the lenses clean. Others are designed to tilt down or away when *Perseverance* is resting or working, to prevent dust from collecting.

shutting it down forever. Astronauts would need to clean any covered equipment, putting them at risk of breathing in the dust themselves.

Because scientists do not know exactly what Martian dust is like, they are testing many different types of dust on Earth. And they are currently testing spacesuit material on Mars. The *Perseverance* rover is carrying five different samples of spacesuit materials. Scientists will test the samples every 3 to 6 months to see how they are holding up.

Super Salty Sea

More than 300 million people on Earth get their water from desalination. The average American uses 80 to 100 gallons (302 to 379 liters) of water a day. It takes 2 gallons (7.6 L) of ocean water to make 1 gallon (3.8 L) of fresh water. The water that is left from desalination is very salty. When dumped right back into the ocean, this ultra-salty water can raise the temperature in that part of the sea. It also decreases the amount of oxygen in the water, which can be deadly to plants and fish. Scientists are trying to find new ways to use the briny waste so it is helpful and not harmful.

Rovers have found plenty of evidence that there is both ice and liquid water on Mars. One of the problems, though, is that it is salty. Humans cannot safely drink saltwater. On Earth, we can use a technique called desalination to remove salt from water. One way to do that is to boil saltwater. The steam is collected. Then it is purified and **condensed** back into water. But desalination can use a lot of energy. The water on Mars might be too salty for desalination. And liquid water changes from a solid to a gas when exposed to Mars's thin atmosphere.

Desalination plants are essential during times of drought. Without them, hot and dry places would need to import water from long distances.

The Future

Being as prepared as possible for life on Mars starts here on Earth. The Hawai'i Space Exploration Analog and Simulation (HI-SEAS) is one place astronauts go to practice. It is funded by NASA and the University of Hawai'i. A 1,200-square-foot (111.5 square meters) dome habitat can hold a team of six. It sits 8,200 feet (2,499 m) above sea level. Its surroundings are similar to the geology of Mars. Crew members behave as though they are actually in space, eating space food and wearing spacesuits outdoors. How people behave in isolation, what kinds of food works best for long-term space missions, and how much direction teams need are a few of the things that were studied.

In 2020, the SENSORIA Program partnered with HI-SEAS. The majority of the participants and mission leaders in the program are female. Their crew members are also early in their research careers and from underrepresented communities.

Imperfect Practice

Teams at HI-SEAS and other simulation sites have been faced with realistic, and sometimes dangerous, situations. The sixth mission was in 2018. It was meant to last for 8 months. But on the fourth day, one member suffered an accidental electric shock. The crew, worried for their teammate's safety, called an ambulance and **evacuated**. The mission was over. But evacuating would not be an option on Mars. It raised some important questions: Is human well-being more important than scientific data? What if not everyone agrees on what to do?

Dirt for growing plants is heavy and takes up a lot of room on a spacecraft. Researchers are testing out growing methods called hydroponics and aeroponics. Hydroponics grows plant roots in liquid. Aeroponics uses a misty air environment.

Thinking about food, water, and oxygen have always been the primary goals when it comes to spaceflight. To send a team to Mars would require around 66,140 pounds (30,000 kg) of food, water, and oxygen supplies. That is much more than what space shuttles can currently handle.

[21ST CENTURY SKILLS LIBRARY]

The soil on Mars is different than the soil on Earth. It also contains a type of salt that is dangerous to people if we eat too much of it. So finding other ways to grow plants is important.

The ESA has been working on the Micro-Ecological Life Support System Alternative (MELiSSA) project since 1987. MELiSSA creates an artificial **ecosystem** that can make those supplies by recycling the waste created by the crew. The waste loops through five different compartments. Good bacteria, algae, and plants work independently to destroy dangerous germs and bacteria. They create water and oxygen and produce a biomass that can be eaten.

Space Snacks

Getting the right amount of calories every day is important. But eating in space is not the same as eating on Earth! Food in space must be lightweight and compact. It also must be sticky or wet. Crumbs will float around. Even salt and pepper come in liquid form. Although one is being tested for future use, there are currently no refrigerators in space, so the food needs to be shelf stable for the entire mission. Astronauts on the ISS get three meals and a snack every day. Foods such as pasta or scrambled eggs can be reheated or rehydrated. Other foods, like brownies or tortillas, can be eaten right out of the package.

More than 50 organizations in 14 countries contribute to MELiSSA. There is a pilot ecosystem located in Barcelona, Spain. In 2019, the first stage of the ecosystem was tested with algae growth on the ISS. Scientists hope to send rats next. The algae creates oxygen and traps carbon dioxide. The rats do the opposite. If that loop works, the MELiSSA team will know they are on the right track. They hope to perfect their life support system by the late 2030s. By then, hopefully the other key pieces to sending humans to Mars will be ready, too.

Fresh fruit, vegetables, candy, and cheese are popular delivery requests by astronauts in space.

Activity: On Board the *SEV*

The *Space Exploration Vehicle* (*SEV*) is about the size of a small pickup. Astronauts will be expected to live, work, and sleep on board. Grab a partner and find out how you would handle cramped quarters.

WHAT YOU'LL NEED:

- **masking tape**
- **measuring tape**

1. Measure out a space on the floor that is 14 1/2-by-6 1/2-feet (4 2/5-by-2 m). Outline the measurements with masking tape. This is about the amount of space inside the *SEV*.

2. Pick a place for your bed. Lay on the floor. Have your partner tape around you. This is your bed space.

3. Repeat step 2, but this time you tape around your partner to make their bed.

4. Spend 30 minutes with your partner in your *SEV* space. Try out things like eating lunch, putting a jacket on and off, eating a snack, working on homework, and doing simple exercises like running in place or doing push-ups.

5. After 30 minutes, record what your experience was like.

6. The *SEV* can hold four people in an emergency. Combine *SEV* space with another pair. Could you do it in real life?

Find Out More

BOOKS

Downs, Mike. *Bringing Space Home.* Vero Beach, FL: Rourke Educational Media, 2021.

Langley, Andrew. *Planet Hunting: Racking Up Data and Looking for Life.* North Mankato, MN: Capstone Press, a Capstone Imprint, 2020.

Lawrence, Ellen. *Living on Mars.* New York, NY: Bearport Publishing, 2019.

Thomas, Rachael L. *Trailblazing Space Scientists.* Minneapolis, MN: Lerner Publications, 2020.

WEBSITES

Facts About Mars
https://www.natgeokids.com/uk/discover/science/space/facts-about-mars
Learn fascinating facts about Mars. Then explore what life might be like in space!

NASA's Mars Exploration Program
https://mars.nasa.gov
The official site of NASA's Mars Exploration Program.

Smithsonian: Exploring Mars
https://www.smithsonianmag.com/science-nature/exploring-mars-180976934
A source for the latest news on NASA, *Perseverance*, *Ingenuity*, and the Red Planet.

Spot the Station: International Space Station
https://spotthestation.nasa.gov
Track the International Space Station's location as it orbits Earth.

GLOSSARY

adapts (uh-DAPTZ) becomes adjusted to new conditions

carbon dioxide (KAR-buhn die-OX-ide) a heavy colorless gas; humans inhale oxygen and exhale carbon dioxide

colonize (KOL-uh-nyz) to send a group of settlers to a new place

condensed (kon-DENST) to change from a gas or vapor to a liquid

core (KOR) the innermost layers of a planet; cores can be solid, liquid, or both

ecosystem (EE-koh-sis-tuhm) a community of living and nonliving things

evacuated (ee-VAK-yoo-ayt-uhd) moved from a place of danger to a safer place

GPS navigation (GEE-PEE-ESS nav-uh-GAY-shuhn) a satellite navigation system that uses satellite signals to find a receiver's position on Earth

orbit (OR-bit) the curved path of an object around a star, planet, or moon

oxidizes (AHX-uh-dyz-uhz) combines with oxygen

particles (PAR-tuh-kuhlz) very small objects

radiation (ray-dee-AY-shuhn) a form of energy that travels through space

rotation (roh-TAY-shuhn) the circular movement of an object around a centered object

satellite (SAT-uh-lite) an artificial body placed in orbit

simulate (sim-yoo-LAY-shuhn) to imitate an event or activity in the real world

unmanned (uhn-MAND) a flight with no crew members on board

INDEX